JN440345

Homo Maskus

Homo Maskus

A collection of new poems by Kim Soo-yeol
Translated by Brother Anthony of Taizé

아시아

Contents

Funeral Flowers 8

A Dandelion 9

Tree and Chair 11

What's That...? 12

Berlin Morning 14

A Day in Copenhagen 16

Fermented Love 18

A Duck 20

Insomnia 22

Aged Sixty 24

Offerings for the Dead 26

In Gaoan Village 28

Last Statement, Rewritten 30

May, Occasional Morning Rain 32
Decalcomania 35
A Beautiful Lifetime 38
Farther than the Moon 42
Keep on Pushing 45
Whistling 47
Homo Maskus 49

Poet's Note 53
The Poet's Essay 57
Commentary 65
What They Say About Kim Soo-yeol 71

HOMO MASKUS

Funeral Flowers

Mourners in black, each clutching the neck of a white flower, standing in front of the deceased person's portrait, shut their eyes and bow their heads, then take one step forward and hesitate briefly whether to put the flower's head facing forward or backward when placing the flowers on the altar, choose what is sensible, draw back one pace and take their leave of the portrait, heads bowed.

Nobody mourns the death of the flowers.

A Dandelion

Puff—

If a spring breeze can come blowing

and carry you flying off

To wherever you want to go,

over the pierced stone walls with their holes,

if you can become a little star

perched above a thatched house,

if you can sparkle yellow,

Then I,

lying prostrate

like this,

after being trampled down, over and over again,
would happily live as shit,
would happily turn into mud
smeared over Grandmother's fingertips.

Tree and Chair

While a dead tree gazes dumbly at the living trees,
the living trees look sadly down on the dead tree.

It was winter, with snow flurries gusting amidst a snow warning.
It was a white day, no one coming, no one going.

While the chair with its empty lap contemplates a tree with a swollen foot,
the tree, dreaming of being a chair, tosses and turns until one dry leaf
settles quietly on the lap of the chair that was once a tree.

What's That...?

A priest
who came to Korea from New Zealand half a century ago
and who once stood at the forefront of the fight against redevelopment
with local residents, and is now retired, serves
as the head of the residents' association in Samyang-dong, Seongbuk-gu.

He is preparing Christmas gift packages
for elderly folk who have a hard time walking.

Two packs of ramyeon,

two packs of seaweed,

one can of tuna,

one can of luncheon meat,

one pack of wet wipes,

one homemade Christmas card...

What on earth is that...?

Once again this year, I'm just passing the year.

Berlin Morning

Berlin city center, the morning commute,
while the traffic lights change and the cars stop

Appearing from somewhere,
dark-skinned, either boyfriend or husband,
standing in the middle of the crossing and juggling to attract attention,
dark-skinned, either girlfriend or wife,
wiping the windshields of the stationary cars, holding out one hand,
saying something to the drivers.

When the traffic light changes, the dark skins get

out of the way of the traffic

and the indifferent cars erase with their wipers

the memory of stopping as they drive off.

The dark-skinned couple's morning passes like that, not earning any tips.

A Day in Copenhagen

Wearing orange coveralls,

those who pick up cigarette butts only pick up cigarette butts

while those with dark skins pushing bikes,

who pick up plastic bottles, only pick up plastic bottles.

The cigarette butt collectors receive a weekly wage from the city government,

those who pick up plastic bottles receive a refund from the mart, at so much per bottle.

Then, in the evening, while the sun hangs in the

middle of the sky,

they mingle with doctors, lawyers and farmers
living in the neighborhood

at an open-air café with canned beer, and talk
about their day.

Fermented Love

Married at twenty,

my old man was nine years older than me.

I didn't know if it was night or day, just worked

and in the meantime raised five kids.

When the time came to stop and smell the roses, he suddenly passed on.

I miss him more as I grow older.

If a flower blooms in a tree, if a persimmon ripens in a persimmon tree, I miss him.

Sons, daughters or whatever, as I grow older, my old man was the best.

Though we didn't live together for long,

I should have left earlier.

If my old man cannot come back, I'd better follow him quickly.

My old man

was so good-looking, I worried someone might take him from me.

I should have left earlier,

but I'm a hunch-backed old woman now.

Will he be able to recognize me?

Wait, where's my comb?

A Duck

A mother, feeling sorry for her pale and ailing little son, bought a duck that had been playing in the water under the West Gate bridge, tied its legs together and hung it from the eaves.

Time passed. Then she took it down as it was flapping, its blood having gone to its head, laid it on a cutting board, and with a kitchen knife sharpened on a whetstone, she cut off its head, collected the red blood gushing out in a china bowl.

The mother mixed it with a digestive tonic and stirred it with her little finger, to keep it from congealing, then after her son held his nose, closed his eyes, and drank it in a single draft, the mother pushed a piece of candy into his soft, red lips as if he had been waiting for that.

Insomnia

I received a tearful text message saying that all the thoughtless guys should gather together on the following afternoon in the container house in the tangerine field of Poet Kim Whatsit from Jocheon for a chicken feast in guise of house-warming.

I can't sleep even if I lie down, I can't fall asleep even if I drink warm milk mixed with salt, it was not until dawn that I split one of the pills I got from the hospital in half and swallowed it, then lay down but still, tossing and turning, I can't get to sleep.

Remembering that evening, the well-cooked

potatoes and the friends sitting around the table, and the steaming hot old hen, as I was going along I bent my fingers, straightened them, bent them and straightened them again,

A rooster crows in the distance.

Aged Sixty

Holding mother's hand, for she has trouble walking,

sometimes pushing father's wheelchair,

we come face to face by chance in the doctor's waiting room,

brush past with an awkward nod.

In a baggy hospital gown,

wearing three-colored slippers, pulling an IV drip

meeting by chance in the smoking room in one corner of the hospital,

when asked: What's the problem? we reply:

So-so, and vaguely look away,

bleak like six in the evening in late autumn.

Receiving notice of the death of a classmate who suddenly went flying away,
I let out a long puff of cigarette smoke like a sigh,
then frowning, slowly, hesitantly, compose
a text message asking someone to pay condolence money on my behalf.

Offerings for the Dead

Every time Father and Mother left for the fields in the early morning, they woke us five kids who were still sleeping and made us promise 'not to forget to prepare Grandfather's food.'

My younger sister, who was taking care of me, and I who was still less dexterous, played merrily outside the gate, then when the sun touched the top of Mount Halla, we ran to the kitchen, prepared barley rice and soup, and offered them up on Grandfather's table in the closet in the inner room.

When Grandfather had finished eating, I offered

up tobacco. In his lifetime, Grandfather's pipe had been very long. While my sister applied her lips to the mouthpiece, I would put tobacco in the bowl and light it with a match, then when sister could not suck for choking, I would suck at the mouthpiece and choke, at which sister would suck again, choke again, and then I would suck ...

Father refrained from smoking for the three years of mourning.

In Gaoan Village

Born in the year of the rat, old Mr. Park, an ethnic Korean living in Gaoan Village, Dongning City, Heilongjiang Province, China, formed an association of one hundred and four people, crossed the river to Russia, then after a year growing tomatoes and cabbages he bought a color television, crossed the river again, dealt in rebars, was swindled by the Russians, incurred a debt of 180,000 yuan, as a last resort went with his wife to Korea to live, worked as a navvy on building sites and paid off the debt after five years,

Their two sons are still in Korea making money,

while the old man has returned to Gaoan Village with his wife and spends time eating snacks and playing mah-jong with the friends still left in the empty village, or crossing the red fields of Manchuria trying in vain to get to sleep.

Last Statement, Rewritten

I, Thomas Ahn Jung-geun, having killed the enemy leader Ito Hirobumi

in my capacity as chief of staff in the Korean Righteous Army,

ask to be treated as a political prisoner, not as a common criminal.

Since Harbin, where I killed the enemy leader,

is a Russian concession, the enemy nation, Japan,

has no authority to judge me.

Take your hands off me, right now.

Ahn Jung-geun, who had written his "Treatise on

Peace in East Asia" in Lushun Prison,

was executed five months after killing the enemy leader.

He was aged thirty-one.

Zhou Enlai, the Chinese prime minister, later said:

—After the Sino-Japanese War, the struggle of the peoples of Korea and China against Japanese imperialism began at the start of this century, when Ahn Jung-geun shot Ito Hirobumi at Harbin station.

May, Occasional Morning Rain

I used the cafeteria of the provincial office as a kitchen.

Having to cook rice for hundreds of people every time,
I was always annoyed when the rice stuck together.
A man running a restaurant nearby
told me to add some salt, so I did,
and the rice became well-cooked.
I felt less apologetic.

I made rice balls because we lacked tableware

and the seasoning was just right.
Women from Yangdong Market and Seobang
Market
brought baskets full of kimchi and gimbap.

The guys from Hyeongje Bakery at Yudong
crossing
each set aside an armful of freshly baked bread.
The men liked red bean bread
while we loved the crust on the soboro bread.

It was drizzling.
It must have been around two in the morning of

the twenty-seventh.

The men said it was dangerous there and we should leave.

We shared out bread and milk as late-night snacks.

and after roughly preparing breakfast

we left the provincial office by the back way.

But, did they, have, breakfast?

Decalcomania

1

On January 24, 1968, in HàMy Village, Vietnam,
the Blue Dragon Unit from Korea
searched every corner, door to door,
and massacred 135 villagers from 30 households.

The bodies mixed with sand were thick with dried blood.
One tiny baby
went crawling up toward its mother's cold breasts,
seeking milk without understanding.

Swarms of ants came crawling over the scorched flesh.

2

On January 17, 1949, in Bukchon-ri, Jocheon-myeon, Jeju-do,

the 2nd Regiment 3rd Battalion of the National Defense Guard

massacred 400 villagers

at the Shrine Field near the elementary school.

The bodies lay tangled at the foot of the surrounding walls,

and one tiny baby

climbed toward its dead mother's dry breasts,

pushed them with its nose and wriggled in confusion.

A flock of crows settled on the bodies scattered by the stone walls.

A Beautiful Lifetime

He now rests in Odeung-dong.
He was originally buried in Geonnip-dong,
but someone used a blunt instrument
to break the gravestone into two pieces.

He had nobody the carry on the family line
and until his death, he
used to check tickets at the Daehan cinema.

Before that, he earned a living
running a tiny rice store in Mugeunseong.

Before that, he was the chief of police at

Seongsanpo.
At the time he was in preventive detention immediately after the Korean War,
he saved lives by claiming that he had not obeyed the order
to shoot 221 people in his jurisdiction because it was wrong.

Before that, he had first come to Jeju Island in 1945 at Liberation
as the first chief of Museulpo Police Station.
During the April 3rd incident, he procured a list of 100 people

from the left-wing leader in his jurisdiction,

encouraged them to surrender, and saved their lives.

Before that he had been in the Independence army.

Immediately after the March 1st Movement, he went into exile in Manchuria,

joined the Citizens' Division, a group within the Independence Movement,

served as commander of the Central Guard and was in the vanguard of the armed struggle.

Born in 1897, died in 1966, his name was Moon Hyeong-sun.

Farther than the Moon
—Kim Si-jong

I was advised by the Osaka Consulate to return to Korea. Knowing that I was preparing a poetry collection about the Gwangju Massacre, they urged me to have it published in Seoul, as if Chun Doo-hwan's officials, who were preparing a visit to Japan, wanted to save his face. But as a survivor of the Jeju 4·3 massacres I could not do that.

At the time of Kim Young-sam, I was invited to the Seoul Writers' Festival, but the consulate demanded that I should sign a pledge to take Korean nationality on my next visit to Korea. As a Joseon nationality holder, I refused. Thanks to the efforts of the organizers, I was still able to attend, but I was only permitted to visit Seoul.

It was finally in the days of President Kim Dae-jung, who began to investigate the facts of the Jeju Uprising, that I was able to visit Jeju for the first time since going to Japan in 1949, with a temporary passport for my Joseon nationality. I was heavy-hearted, felt ashamed to meet the comrades who had suffered during the Uprising. “Welcome home!” I was saved by the way my niece cried as she hugged me.

Two graves lay huddled side by side beneath thick thorns, the graves of my parents who had died forty years before. I saw them for the first time. I knelt down and wept like a calf. Wishing to be able to visit the graves every year for the rest of my life, I took Korean nationality in 2003. In that year, the newly installed President Roh Moo-hyun officially apologized for the Jeju Incident, acknowledging it as "a fault of state power."

Half a century since I went to Japan, Jeju was far away,

it was farther away than the moon.

Keep on Pushing

Dear Professor Dawkins,

I am writing because I have to be absent on Friday.

I have to join my friends in the climate change march in London.

Because I think climate change is a very serious matter.

Beginning in Europe, the strike by schoolchildren all over the world stems from a single-person protest in front of the Swedish parliament building by Greta Thunberg, who looks like Pippi Longstocking, calling for adults to take an interest in climate change.

While the British Prime Minister said that it was a waste of time and that students should "put study first," Pope Francesco prayed, "Keep on pushing," in an interview with her.

She became the youngest person ever nominated for the Nobel Peace Prize.

Still now, on Fridays, young people all over the world take to the streets instead of going to school.

Whistling

1.

Due to Covid 19 a nine-year-old boy who said he wanted to see his friends though he could not go to school abruptly met his end, bestowing new life on seven people, then went to heaven. He liked to share with friends, whether it was cookies or games, and he especially loved to whistle. His Mother sends him a last message:

2.

Thank you for being born as my son.

I will love you in the future, too,

I'll remember you for the rest of my life.

If I hear someone whistling in the distance,

I'll live on, believing that you are coming.

I love you and thank you

Homo Maskus

Only indoors is above water.

Leaving home means plunging into the water.

There's no entering the water without a mask.

You may not. If you meet a mask coming toward you

you have to keep your distance or endure a fierce glare.

You can't use public transport or drink a cup of tea.

Not only men and women, but even the young and old are no exception.

Mask talks to mask,

mask and mask talk more loudly because of the

masks.

An extra mask is salvation and God's grace.

Outdoors is always deep under water

The masks flutter in the wind.

Masks flutter on leafless branches.

Red masks, blue masks, yellow masks, black masks,

everyone is wearing a mask except for the sniffer dogs at the airport.

Not only passengers, but also airplanes are wearing masks.

The stone Harubang at the airport is no exception.

The masks attract the wind and roll about like fallen leaves.

Pigeons in the park stagger about, their feet caught in masks.

Instead of jellyfish, masks get drawn up in old fishermen's nets.

Nowadays, sixty billion chicken bones form strata each year.

Today, it's only when you're indoors that you can take off your mask and exhale.

POET'S NOTE

While walking about here and there, I collected scribbled notes.

They are records of time spent roaming freely.

Will such days come again?

The year that started with masks is ending with masks.

How often have I left my mask behind and had to go back for it?

Looking back, it's all my fault.

The past days of heedless living are observing my behavior closely today.

I have nothing to say.

I have to sit quietly and learn to read the world.

THE POET'S ESSAY

A Walker's Day

A bird flies down and perches on the empty pots on the veranda.

It looks around, peers here and there, then flies away.

I wonder if it's the bird that came before, but a cat lazily appears.

It rubs its body against the screening, meows once or twice,

and when there is no reply, it slowly vanishes again.

I leave the house.

Putting water into a thermos, putting on a hat, and taking a stick···

Then I come back. Putting on a mask, I set off again.

One thousand six hundred steps to the bus stop.

I ignore a bus headed to Jeju University and get on one going to Seogwipo.

Both the driver and the people on the bus are masks.

A new mask searches hesitantly for an empty seat and sits down.

The bus leaves.

It passes Namguksa, where it is said that the tea tastes excellent.

After passing a university hospital where stooping elderly folk get on and off,

it passes Sancheondan, that claims to be the last convenience store.

After passing the nursing hospital, it passes Yangji Park, where my father lies

and I get off at Halla Eco Forest.

I walk along the Sutmoru forest trail. Birdsong accompanies me.

The beauty of the forest trail lies in its tranquility.

Even that only lasts for a while,

Squawk! Squawk! Squawk!

a pheasant, startled by the presence of people, goes soaring up.

A deer, startled by the pheasant's cry, hides its behind.

I enter Jeolmul Forest Park.

I think of heading for Saetgae Ori-oreum, but finally I choose the path around it.

I prefer a natural dirt track to tidy stairs.

The purple fruits of the mulberry tree on the dirt road greet me.

Just as I am losing my breath, I finally reach the cypress forest.

I have to rest here for a moment.

That way, I feel less sorry for the benches disposed here.

A sip of warm water spreads through my body.

Over there people who reached the benches first are resting.

After drinking the water, I put on the mask again.

Where are those people who visited this forest every day last summer

in order to heal their sick bodies?

I hurry on again.

After passing the cypress forest, here is the luxuriant cedar forest.

A sound of chanting drifts from a small hermitage selling garlic bean-paste.

That means that I am almost at the end of the forest road.

Now, once snow falls on Jeolmul Oreum,

the wind blows, and the crows cry,

soon, a host of pinks will bloom through the snow.

After taking a sip of cool spring water from Jeolmul,

I leave Jeolmul Recreational Forest and head for the Bus Stop.

There's no one there, perhaps a bus has just left.

Looking at the timetable, I have to wait thirty minutes for the next bus.

I take out my phone and look at the pedometer, nine thousand steps.

I have to walk a little more to reach ten thousand steps.

I think of walking around some more but change my mind.

After boarding the bus, I get off one stop early

and have a drink of makgeolli with haejangguk.

Now I have to go to my house, that birds and cats sometimes visit.

Staggering a little.

COMMENTARY

The sound of age sixty exhaling on reaching deceptive appearances

Hong Ki-Don
(Literary Critic, Professor at Catholic University)

The world of things that have not yet come

With the coronavirus, interest in and demand for a new normal are increasing. Our poet seems to be laying the groundwork for this new normal, beginning with the possibility of coexistence with nature. This can be confirmed in "Homo Maskus", and "Keep on Pushing." "Homo Maskus" introduces a symmetry between the world outdoors and that under water. Like a haenyeo, who has to endure life and death by herself in the sea, the homo maskus outside the house must each seek their own survival and are even hostile to others. In addition, humans are selfish enough to focus only on their own survival problems and not extend consideration to other beings. "Pigeons in the park stagger about, their feet caught in masks. Instead of jellyfish, masks get drawn up in old fishermen's nets."

A leap forward to the postmodern will be possible in the midst of such advice and reflection. "Keep on Pushing" is a message from Pope Francis, supporting Greta Thunberg. Since this was used as the title of a poem, the pope's message is transferred directly to the voice of the poet.

"Funeral Flowers," "A Dandelion," and "Tree and Chair" contain thoughts on the relationship between life and death. "Funeral Flowers" is a poem that evokes the "death of flowers" that takes place in order to mourn the death of a human being.

It is remarkable that the effect is emphasized by anthropomorphizing the flowers with the expression "clutching the neck of a white flower." "A Dandelion" reveals the aspects of life unfolding through death, referring to dandelion seeds and dandelion flowers as you and me, respectively. By saying "if you can become a little star perched above a thatched house, if you can sparkle yellow," life is established by a rising image, and death in contrast by a descending image, "Then I, lying prostrate like this, after being trampled down over and over again, would happily live as shit, would happily turn into mud smeared over Grandmother's fingertips." While "A Dandelion" takes death as nourishment and captures the rising aspect of life, "Tree and Chair" contains the mutuality of life and death. At first, the poet seems to be negatively grasping the death he will face someday. The first lines, "While a dead tree gazes dumbly at the living trees, the living trees look sadly down on the dead tree" reveals this. However, when it reaches the point of pure whiteness ("a white day") that has abolished all desire, perception changes. The dead tree, shaped into a "chair with its empty lap," can be free from all desire. For example, the act of kneeling may represent surrender, but it can also represent surprise and joy, but how did the dead tree empty its knees to form an empty lap? In addition, the living tree is said to be "a tree with a swollen foot", which highlights its hardships. The mutuality of life and death ends with the following passage: "the tree, dreaming of being a chair, tosses and turns until one dry leaf settles quietly on the lap of the chair that was once a tree."

The poems of things that have not yet come may also be related to the poet's age, sixty. These poems gauge the future based on the years that the poet has lived and unfold thoughts on the death that does not feel far away. In this way, the poet endures, feeling "bleak like six in the evening in late autumn."

WHAT THEY SAY ABOUT KIM SOO-YEOL

Kim Soo-yeol's poems preserve well the language of Jeju Island, the poet's birthplace, while taking care not to sound too unfamiliar for readers. Their gaze as they contemplate social and historical realities, including the Jeju Incident, is sharp and warm.

Jeong Hee-seong (Poet)

In a world where everything is focused on the center and even literature is mainly written in the language of Seoul, Kim Soo-yeol's bold introduction of the Jeju language into his poems is to be highly appreciated.

Bok Hyo-geun (Poet)

Poet Kim Soo-yeol's poems do not let go of affection for the world, but constantly ask fundamental questions intended to reorganize the world. I value highly his poetic contribution to the overall history of Korean literature.

Shin Kyeong-rim (Poet)

K-POET
Homo Maskus

Written by Kim Soo-yeol | **Translated by** Brother Anthony of Taizé
Published by ASIA Publishers | 445, Hoedong-gil, Paju-si, Gyeonggi-do, Korea
(Seoul Office: 161-1, Seodal-ro, Dongjak-gu, Seoul, Korea)
Homepage Address www.bookasia.org | **Tel** (822).821.5055 | **Fax** (822).821.5057
ISBN 979-11-5662-317-5 (set) | 979-11-5662-527-8
First published in Korea by ASIA Publishers 2020

This book is published with the support of the Literature Translation Institute of Korea (LTI Korea).

K-픽션 한국 젊은 소설

최근에 발표된 단편소설 중 가장 우수하고 흥미로운 작품을 엄선하여 출간하는 〈K-픽션〉은 한국문학의 생생한 현장을 국내외 독자들과 실시간으로 공유하고자 기획되었습니다. 원작의 재미와 품격을 최대한 살린 〈K-픽션〉 시리즈는 매 계절마다 새로운 작품을 선보입니다.

001 버핏과의 저녁 식사-**박민규** Dinner with Buffett-**Park Min-gyu**
002 아르판-**박형서** Arpan-**Park hyoung su**
003 애드벌룬-**손보미** Hot Air Balloon-**Son Bo-mi**
004 나의 클린트 이스트우드-**오한기** My Clint Eastwood-**Oh Han-ki**
005 이베리아의 전갈-**최민우** Dishonored-**Choi Min-woo**
006 양의 미래-**황정은** Kong's Garden-**Hwang Jung-eun**
007 대니-**윤이형** Danny-**Yun I-hyeong**
008 퇴근-**천명관** Homecoming-**Cheon Myeong-kwan**
009 옥화-**금희** Ok-hwa-**Geum Hee**
010 시차-**백수린** Time Difference-**Baik Sou linne**
011 올드 맨 리버-**이장욱** Old Man River-**Lee Jang-wook**
012 권순찬과 착한 사람들-**이기호** Kwon Sun-chan and Nice People-**Lee Ki-ho**
013 알바생 자르기-**장강명** Fired-**Chang Kangmyoung**
014 어디로 가고 싶으신가요-**김애란** Where Would You Like To Go?-**Kim Ae-ran**
015 세상에서 가장 비싼 소설-**김민정** The World's Most Expensive Novel-**Kim Min-jung**
016 체스의 모든 것-**김금희** Everything About Chess-**Kim Keum-hee**
017 할로윈-**정한아** Halloween-**Chung Han-ah**
018 그 여름-**최은영** The Summer-**Choi Eunyoung**
019 어느 피씨주의자의 종생기-**구병모** The Story of P.C.-**Gu Byeong-mo**
020 모르는 영역-**권여선** An Unknown Realm-**Kwon Yeo-sun**
021 4월의 눈-**손원평** April Snow-**Sohn Won-pyung**
022 서우-**강화길** Seo-u-**Kang Hwa-gil**
023 가출-**조남주** Run Away-**Cho Nam-joo**
024 연애의 감정학-**백영옥** How to Break Up Like a Winner-**Baek Young-ok**
025 창모-**우다영** Chang-mo-**Woo Da-young**
026 검은 방-**정지아** The Black Room-**Jeong Ji-a**
027 도쿄의 마야-**장류진** Maya in Tokyo-**Jang Ryu-jin**
028 홀리데이 홈-**편혜영** Holiday Home-**Pyun Hye-young**

바이링궐 에디션 한국 대표 소설

한국문학의 가장 중요하고 첨예한 문제의식을 가진 작가들의 대표작을 주제별로 선정!
하버드 한국학 연구원 및 세계 각국의 한국문학 전문 번역진이 참여한 번역 시리즈!
미국 하버드대학교와 컬럼비아대학교 동아시아학과, 캐나다 브리티시컬럼비아대학교 아시아학과 등 해외 대학에서 교재로 채택!

바이링궐 에디션 한국 대표 소설 set 1

분단 Division

01 병신과 머저리-**이청준** The Wounded-**Yi Cheong-jun**
02 어둠의 혼-**김원일** Soul of Darkness-**Kim Won-il**
03 순이삼촌-**현기영** Sun-i Samch'on-**Hyun Ki-young**
04 엄마의 말뚝 1-**박완서** Mother's Stake I-**Park Wan-suh**
05 유형의 땅-**조정래** The Land of the Banished-**Jo Jung-rae**

산업화 Industrialization

06 무진기행-**김승옥** Record of a Journey to Mujin-**Kim Seung-ok**
07 삼포 가는 길-**황석영** The Road to Sampo-**Hwang Sok-yong**
08 아홉 켤레의 구두로 남은 사내-**윤흥길** The Man Who Was Left as Nine Pairs of Shoes-**Yun Heung-gil**
09 돌아온 우리의 친구-**신상웅** Our Friend's Homecoming-**Shin Sang-ung**
10 원미동 시인-**양귀자** The Poet of Wŏnmi-dong-**Yang Kwi-ja**

여성 Women

11 중국인 거리-**오정희** Chinatown-**Oh Jung-hee**
12 풍금이 있던 자리-**신경숙** The Place Where the Harmonium Was-**Shin Kyung-sook**
13 하나코는 없다-**최윤** The Last of Hanak'o-**Ch'oe Yun**
14 인간에 대한 예의-**공지영** Human Decency-**Gong Ji-young**
15 빈처-**은희경** Poor Man's Wife-**Eun Hee-kyung**

바이링궐 에디션 한국 대표 소설 set 2

자유 Liberty

16 필론의 돼지-**이문열** Pilon's Pig-**Yi Mun-yol**
17 슬로우 불릿-**이대환** Slow Bullet-**Lee Dae-hwan**
18 직선과 독가스-**임철우** Straight Lines and Poison Gas-**Lim Chul-woo**
19 깃발-**홍희담** The Flag-**Hong Hee-dam**
20 새벽 출정-**방현석** Off to Battle at Dawn-**Bang Hyeon-seok**

사랑과 연애 Love and Love Affairs

21 별을 사랑하는 마음으로-**윤후명** With the Love for the Stars-**Yun Hu-myong**
22 목련공원-**이승우** Magnolia Park-**Lee Seung-u**
23 칼에 찔린 자국-**김인숙** Stab-**Kim In-suk**
24 회복하는 인간-**한강** Convalescence-**Han Kang**
25 트렁크-**정이현** In the Trunk-**Jeong Yi-hyun**

남과 북 South and North

26 판문점-**이호철** Panmunjom-**Yi Ho-chol**
27 수난 이대-**하근찬** The Suffering of Two Generations-**Ha Geun-chan**
28 분지-**남정현** Land of Excrement-**Nam Jung-hyun**
29 봄 실상사-**정도상** Spring at Silsangsa Temple-**Jeong Do-sang**
30 은행나무 사랑-**김하기** Gingko Love-**Kim Ha-kee**

바이링궐 에디션 한국 대표 소설 set 3

서울 Seoul

31 눈사람 속의 검은 항아리-**김소진** The Dark Jar within the Snowman-**Kim So-jin**
32 오후, 가로지르다-**하성란** Traversing Afternoon-**Ha Seong-nan**
33 나는 봉천동에 산다-**조경란** I Live in Bongcheon-dong-**Jo Kyung-ran**
34 그렇습니까? 기린입니다-**박민규** Is That So? I'm A Giraffe-**Park Min-gyu**
35 성탄특선-**김애란** Christmas Specials-**Kim Ae-ran**

전통 Tradition

36 무자년의 가을 사흘-**서정인** Three Days of Autumn, 1948-**Su Jung-in**
37 유자소전-**이문구** A Brief Biography of Yuja-**Yi Mun-gu**
38 향기로운 우물 이야기-**박범신** The Fragrant Well-**Park Bum-shin**
39 월행-**송기원** A Journey under the Moonlight-**Song Ki-won**
40 협죽도 그늘 아래-**성석제** In the Shade of the Oleander-**Song Sok-ze**

아방가르드 Avant-garde

41 아겔다마-**박상륭** Akeldama-**Park Sang-ryoong**
42 내 영혼의 우물-**최인석** A Well in My Soul-**Choi In-seok**
43 당신에 대해서-**이인성** On You-**Yi In-seong**
44 회색 時-**배수아** Time In Gray-**Bae Su-ah**
45 브라운 부인-**정영문** Mrs. Brown-**Jung Young-moon**

바이링궐 에디션 한국 대표 소설 set 4

디아스포라 Diaspora

46 속옷-**김남일** Underwear-**Kim Nam-il**
47 상하이에 두고 온 사람들-**공선옥** People I Left in Shanghai-**Gong Sun-ok**
48 모두에게 복된 새해-**김연수** Happy New Year to Everyone-**Kim Yeon-su**
49 코끼리-**김재영** The Elephant-**Kim Jae-young**
50 먼지별-**이경** Dust Star-**Lee Kyung**

가족 Family

51 혜자의 눈꽃-**천승세** Hye-ja's Snow-Flowers-**Chun Seung-sei**
52 아베의 가족-**전상국** Ahbe's Family-**Jeon Sang-guk**
53 문 앞에서-**이동하** Outside the Door-**Lee Dong-ha**
54 그리고, 축제-**이혜경** And Then the Festival-**Lee Hye-kyung**
55 봄밤-**권여선** Spring Night-**Kwon Yeo-sun**

유머 Humor

56 오늘의 운세-**한창훈** Today's Fortune-**Han Chang-hoon**
57 새-**전성태** Bird-**Jeon Sung-tae**
58 밀수록 다시 가까워지는-**이기호** So Far, and Yet So Near-**Lee Ki-ho**
59 유리방패-**김중혁** The Glass Shield-**Kim Jung-hyuk**
60 전당포를 찾아서-**김종광** The Pawnshop Chase-**Kim Chong-kwang**

바이링궐 에디션 한국 대표 소설 set 5

관계 Relationship

61 도둑견습 – **김주영** Robbery Training-**Kim Joo-young**
62 사랑하라, 희망 없이 – **윤영수** Love, Hopelessly-**Yun Young-su**
63 봄날 오후, 과부 셋 – **정지아** Spring Afternoon, Three Widows-**Jeong Ji-a**
64 유턴 지점에 보물지도를 묻다 - **윤성희** Burying a Treasure Map at the U-turn-**Yoon Sung-hee**
65 쁘이거나 쯔이거나 - **백가흠** Puy, Thuy, Whatever-**Paik Ga-huim**

일상의 발견 Discovering Everyday Life

66 나는 음식이다 – **오수연** I Am Food-**Oh Soo-yeon**
67 트럭 – **강영숙** Truck-**Kang Young-sook**
68 통조림 공장 - **편혜영** The Canning Factory-**Pyun Hye-young**
69 꽃 – **부희령** Flowers-**Pu Hee-ryoung**
70 피의일요일 – **윤이형** BloodySunday-**Yun I-hyeong**

금기와 욕망 Taboo and Desire

71 북소리 - **송영** Drumbeat-**Song Yong**
72 발칸의 장미를 내게 주었네 - **정미경** He Gave Me Roses of the Balkans-**Jung Mi-kyung**
73 아무도 돌아오지 않는 밤 – **김숨** The Night Nobody Returns Home-**Kim Soom**
74 젓가락여자 – **천운영** Chopstick Woman-**Cheon Un-yeong**
75 아직 일어나지 않은 일 – **김미월** What Has Yet to Happen-**Kim Mi-wol**

바이링궐 에디션 한국 대표 소설 set 6

운명 Fate

76 언니를 놓치다 – **이경자** Losing a Sister-**Lee Kyung-ja**
77 아들 – **윤정모** Father and Son-**Yoon Jung-mo**
78 명두 – **구효서** Relics-**Ku Hyo-seo**
79 모독 – **조세희** Insult-**Cho Se-hui**
80 화요일의 강 – **손홍규** Tuesday River-**Son Hong-gyu**

미의 사제들 Aesthetic Priests

81 고수 – **이외수** Grand Master-**Lee Oisoo**
82 말을 찾아서 – **이순원** Looking for a Horse-**Lee Soon-won**
83 상춘곡 – **윤대녕** Song of Everlasting Spring-**Youn Dae-nyeong**
84 삭매와 자미 – **김별아** Sakmae and Jami-**Kim Byeol-ah**
85 저만치 혼자서 – **김훈** Alone Over There-**Kim Hoon**

식민지의 벌거벗은 자들 The Naked in the Colony

86 감자 – **김동인** Potatoes-**Kim Tong-in**
87 운수 좋은 날 – **현진건** A Lucky Day-**Hyŏn Chin'gŏn**
88 탈출기 – **최서해** Escape-**Ch'oe So-hae**
89 과도기 – **한설야** Transition-**Han Seol-ya**
90 지하촌 – **강경애** The Underground Village-**Kang Kyŏng-ae**

바이링궐 에디션 한국 대표 소설 set 7

백치가 된 식민지 지식인 Colonial Intellectuals Turned "Idiots"

91 날개 – **이상** Wings-**Yi Sang**
92 김 강사와 T 교수 – **유진오** Lecturer Kim and Professor T-**Chin-O Yu**
93 소설가 구보씨의 일일 – **박태원** A Day in the Life of Kubo the Novelist-**Pak Taewon**
94 비 오는 길 – **최명익** Walking in the Rain-**Ch'oe Myŏngik**
95 빛 속에 – **김사량** Into the Light-**Kim Sa-ryang**

한국의 잃어버린 얼굴 Traditional Korea's Lost Faces

96 봄·봄 – **김유정** Spring, Spring–**Kim Yu-jeong**
97 벙어리 삼룡이 – **나도향** Samnyong the Mute–**Na Tohyang**
98 달밤 – **이태준** An Idiot's Delight–**Yi T'ae-jun**
99 사랑손님과 어머니 – **주요섭** Mama and the Boarder–**Chu Yo-sup**
100 갯마을 – **오영수** Seaside Village–**Oh Yeongsu**

해방 전후(前後) Before and After Liberation

101 소망 – **채만식** Juvesenility–**Ch'ae Man-Sik**
102 두 파산 – **염상섭** Two Bankruptcies–**Yom Sang-Seop**
103 풀잎 – **이효석** Leaves of Grass–**Lee Hyo-seok**
104 맥 – **김남천** Barley–**Kim Namch'on**
105 꺼삐딴 리 – **전광용** Kapitan Ri–**Chŏn Kwangyong**

전후(戰後) Korea After the Korean War

106 소나기 – **황순원** The Cloudburst–**Hwang Sun-Won**
107 등신불 – **김동리** Tŭngsin-bul–**Kim Tong-ni**
108 요한 시집 – **장용학** The Poetry of John–**Chang Yong-hak**
109 비 오는 날 – **손창섭** Rainy Days–**Son Chang-sop**
110 오발탄 – **이범선** A Stray Bullet–**Lee Beomseon**